Ages 2-5

I SPY
BEACH

BOOK FOR KIDS

COPYRIGHT @ 2023

I Spy With My Little Eye Something Beginning With...

A

Is

Airplane

I Spy With My Little Eye Something Beginning With...

B Is Boat

I Spy With My Little Eye Something Beginning With...

C

Is

Coconut

I Spy With My Little Eye Something Beginning With...

D

Is

Dragonfly

I Spy With My Little Eye Something Beginning With...

E

I Is

Eagle

I Spy With My Little Eye Something Beginning With...

F

Is

Fish

I SPY With My Little Eye Something Beginning With...

G Is Garden

I Spy With My Little Eye Something Beginning With...

H
I Is
Hammock

I Spy With My Little Eye Something Beginning With...

I

I is

Ice Cream

I Spy With My Little Eye Something Beginning With...

J

Is

Juice

I Spy With My Little Eye Something Beginning With...

K

Is

Kayak

I Spy With My Little Eye Something Beginning With...

L

Is

Lighthouse

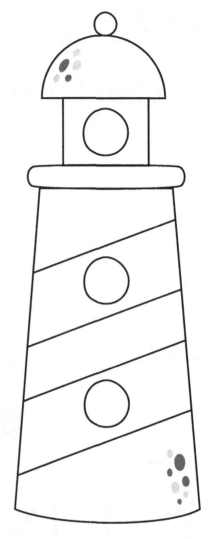

I Spy With My Little Eye Something Beginning With...

M

Is

Mango

I Spy With My Little Eye Something Beginning With...

N
Is
Narwhal

I Spy With My Little Eye Something Beginning With...

O

Is

Orange

I Spy With My Little Eye Something Beginning With...

P

I is

Pineapple

I Spy With My Little Eye Something Beginning With...

Q

Is

Queen

I Spy With My Little Eye Something Beginning With...

R

I Is

Rose

I Spy With My Little Eye Something Beginning With...

S Is Sunflower

I SPY With My Little Eye Something Beginning With...

T

I Is

T Tomato

I Spy With My Little Eye Something Beginning With...

U
Is
Unicorn

I SPY With My Little Eye Something Beginning With...

V

Is

Vase

I Spy With My Little Eye Something Beginning With...

W

Is

Whale

I Spy With My Little Eye Something Beginning With...

X

Is

X-ray fish

I Spy With My Little Eye Something Beginning With...

Y

Is

Yacht

I Spy With My Little Eye Something Beginning With...

Z
Is
Zinnia

Made in United States
North Haven, CT
30 April 2023